Piano • Vocal • Guitar

STEVEN CURTIS CHAPMAN
THIS MOMENT

ISBN-13: 978-1-4234-5283-6
ISBN-10: 1-4234-5283-6

HAL•LEONARD®
CORPORATION
7777 W. BLUEMOUND RD. P.O. BOX 13819 MILWAUKEE, WI 53213

Visit Hal Leonard Online at
www.halleonard.com

www.stevencurtischapman.com

MIRACLE OF THE MOMENT

Words and Music by STEVEN CURTIS CHAPMAN
and MATT BRONLEEWE

Pop Rock

It's time for let - ting go ____ what's
one who knows ____

all of our ____ "if on - ly's" 'cause we don't have ____ a time ____ ma - chine. ____
real - ly out ____ there wait - ing in all the mo - ments yet ____ to be. ____

And e - ven if we did, ____ would we
And all we need to know ____

BROKEN

Words and Music by
STEVEN CURTIS CHAPMAN

Recorded a half step lower.

CINDERELLA

Words and Music by
STEVEN CURTIS CHAPMAN

So she'll be gone. She will be gone.

D.S. al Coda

CODA

YOURS

Words and Music by STEVEN CURTIS CHAPMAN
and JONAS MYRIN

Bb/F

F

-da,
-ville

I see the scars ___ that war has left be-
like Sing- a- pore, ___ Ma- nil - a and Shang-

Bb/F

F

hind.
hai.

Hope like ___ the sun is fad-
I brushed by ___ the beg- gar's ___ hand ___ and the

Bb/F

F

-ing
wealth - y man, ___

and they're wait- ing for ___ a cure ___ no one can
and ev- 'ry- where ___ I look ___ I re - a-

Bb/F

Bb

find.
lize

And I hear ___ chil - dren's voic - es sing-
that, just like ___ the streets ___ of Lon -

SOMETHING CRAZY

Words and Music by STEVEN CURTIS CHAPMAN
and MATT BRONLEEWE

Recorded a half step lower.

real - ly think _ an - y - bod - y wants _ to hear _ what he has to say? _ He's not
drive a Beam - er, but I've nev - er seen _ her an - y hap - pi - er than she is now. _ I met them

scream-ing at an - y - bod - y; in fact, _ he says it's a love sto - ry that he's try-ing to tell _ them. And he
all _ a-round the world; they're the boys _ and the girls _ filled up _ with the love of the Fa - ther. And they

knows he may _ look a lit - tle strange, _ but he just smiles _ and says,
know they may _ look a lit - tle strange, _ but they just smile _ and say,

D.S. al Coda

cra - zy but it's true, _ you real-ly don't know love at all __ till it's mak-ing you do...

CODA

mak - ing you do some - thing cra - zy.

CHILDREN OF GOD

Words and Music by
STEVEN CURTIS CHAPMAN

Driving Rock

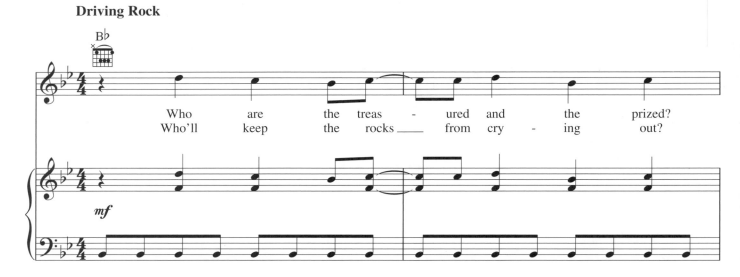

Who are the treas - ured and the prized?
Who'll keep the rocks ___ from cry - ing out?

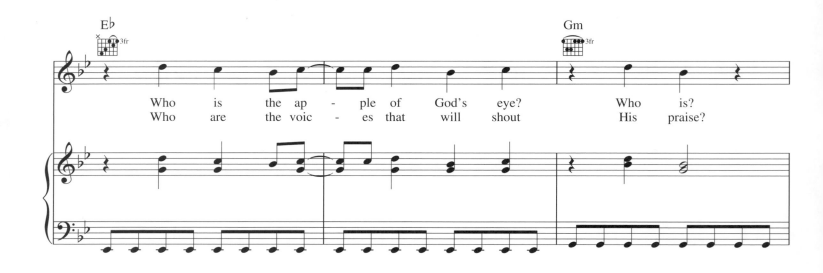

Who is the ap - ple of God's eye? Who is?
Who are the voic - es that will shout His praise?

We are, we are, we are. Who are the ones ___ who bear His name?
We are, we are, we are. Who are the ones ___ who bear His name?

ONE HEARTBEAT AT A TIME

Words and Music by
STEVEN CURTIS CHAPMAN

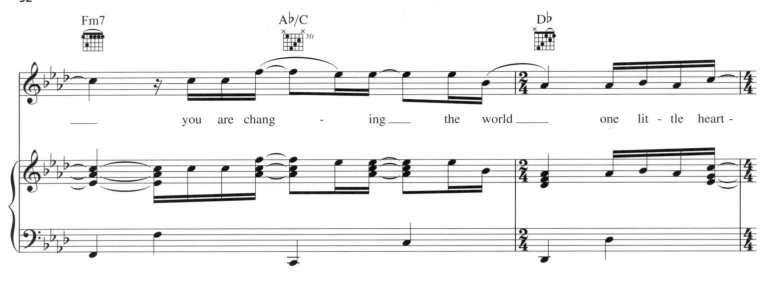

you are chang - ing___ the world___ one lit - tle heart -

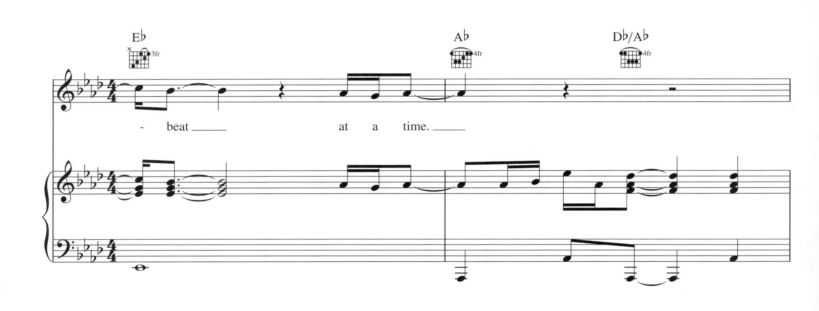

- beat ___ at a time. ___

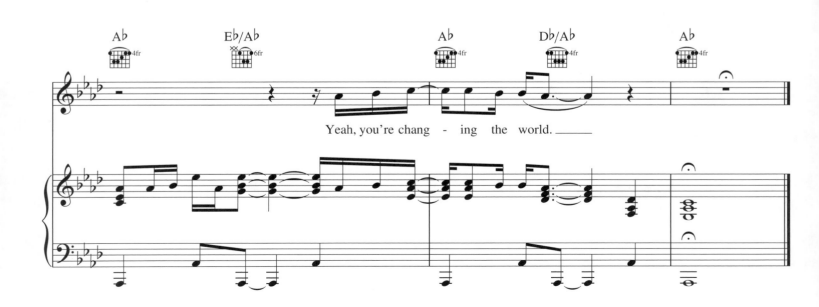

Yeah, you're chang - ing the world. ___

MY SURRENDER

Words and Music by STEVEN CURTIS CHAPMAN
and MATT BRONLEEWE

Recorded a half step higher.

YOU ARE BEING LOVED

Words and Music by
STEVEN CURTIS CHAPMAN

Moderately fast Rock

So you think love ___ is on-ly for the good ___

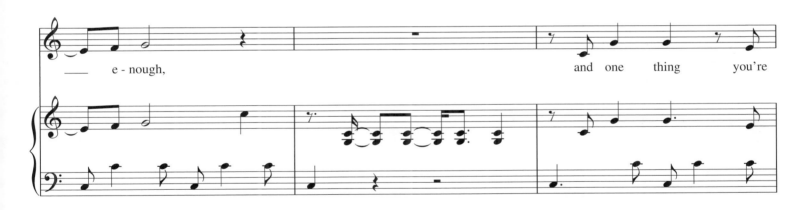

___ e - nough, and one thing you're

nev - er gon - na be ___ wor - thy of. But

Recorded a half step higher.

DEFINITION OF ME

Words and Music by
STEVEN CURTIS CHAPMAN

70

WITH ONE VOICE

Words and Music by STEVEN CURTIS CHAPMAN
and MATT REDMAN